"Wherever you are, be
there totally."

- Eckhart Tolle

# The Body Scan

The body scan is a popular tool for meditation and mindfulness. The reader relaxes peacefully, usually lying down or reclining. They then meditate on different areas of their body in turn, observing any sensations they may be experiencing. This can be a calming and relaxing way to meditate, but it may also train awareness of senses, allowing the person meditating to be more aware, mindful and accepting of their sensorial experience, ultimately learning to be more 'in the present.'

# Body Scan

Today's Date _____     Time _____

Where are you? _____

## Head and Face

[ ]

## Chest

[ ]

## Neck and Shoulders

[ ]

## Stomach

[ ]

## Spine

[ ]

## Arms

[ ]

## Hips and Pelvis

[ ]

## Legs

[ ]

## Whole body sensations

[ ]

### Sensations

Warm - Cold - Soft - Hard -Breeze - Damp - Dry

Tense - Strong - Taut - Numb - Tingling - Tickling - Muscle - Slender - Fragile

Pressure - Throbbing - Blocked - Pulse - Stabbing - Quivering

Nauseous - Shaking - Aching - Breathless - Wired - Anxious

Soothed - Relaxed - Comfortable - Free Flowing

# Body Scan

Today's Date _____     Time _____

Where are you? _____

## Head and Face

## Chest

## Neck and Shoulders

## Stomach

## Spine

## Arms

## Hips and Pelvis

## Legs

## Whole body sensations

### Sensations

Warm - Cold - Soft - Hard -Breeze - Damp - Dry

Tense - Strong - Taut - Numb - Tingling - Tickling - Muscle - Slender - Fragile

Pressure - Throbbing - Blocked - Pulse - Stabbing - Quivering

Nauseous - Shaking - Aching - Breathless - Wired - Anxious

Soothed - Relaxed - Comfortable - Free Flowing

# Body Scan

Today's Date _____     Time _____

Where are you? _____

Head and Face

[ ]

Chest

[ ]

Neck and Shoulders

[ ]

Stomach

[ ]

Spine

[ ]

Arms

[ ]

Hips and Pelvis

[ ]

Legs

[ ]

Whole body sensations

[ ]

## Sensations

Warm - Cold - Soft - Hard -Breeze - Damp - Dry

Tense - Strong - Taut - Numb - Tingling - Tickling - Muscle - Slender - Fragile

Pressure - Throbbing - Blocked - Pulse - Stabbing - Quivering

Nauseous - Shaking - Aching - Breathless - Wired - Anxious

Soothed - Relaxed - Comfortable - Free Flowing

# Body Scan

Today's Date _____    Time _____

Where are you? _____

### Head and Face

 

### Chest

 

### Neck and Shoulders

 

### Stomach

 

### Spine

 

### Arms

 

### Hips and Pelvis

 

### Legs

 

### Whole body sensations

 

## Sensations

Warm - Cold - Soft - Hard -Breeze - Damp - Dry

Tense - Strong - Taut - Numb - Tingling - Tickling - Muscle - Slender - Fragile

Pressure - Throbbing - Blocked - Pulse - Stabbing - Quivering

Nauseous - Shaking - Aching - Breathless - Wired - Anxious

Soothed - Relaxed - Comfortable - Free Flowing

# Body Scan

Today's Date _____          Time _____

Where are you? _____

**Head and Face**

[ ]

**Chest**

[ ]

**Neck and Shoulders**

[ ]

**Stomach**

[ ]

**Spine**

[ ]

**Arms**

[ ]

**Hips and Pelvis**

[ ]

**Legs**

[ ]

**Whole body sensations**

[ ]

### Sensations

Warm - Cold - Soft - Hard -Breeze - Damp - Dry

Tense - Strong - Taut - Numb - Tingling - Tickling - Muscle - Slender - Fragile

Pressure - Throbbing - Blocked - Pulse - Stabbing - Quivering

Nauseous - Shaking - Aching - Breathless - Wired - Anxious

Soothed - Relaxed - Comfortable - Free Flowing

# Body Scan

Today's Date _____     Time _____

Where are you? _____

## Head and Face

## Chest

## Neck and Shoulders

## Stomach

## Spine

## Arms

## Hips and Pelvis

## Legs

## Whole body sensations

### Sensations

Warm - Cold - Soft - Hard -Breeze - Damp - Dry

Tense - Strong - Taut - Numb - Tingling - Tickling - Muscle - Slender - Fragile

Pressure - Throbbing - Blocked - Pulse - Stabbing - Quivering

Nauseous - Shaking - Aching - Breathless - Wired - Anxious

Soothed - Relaxed - Comfortable - Free Flowing

# Body Scan  Today's Date _____  Time _____

Where are you? _____

Head and Face

Chest

Neck and Shoulders

Stomach

Spine

Arms

Hips and Pelvis

Legs

Whole body sensations

Sensations

Warm - Cold - Soft - Hard -Breeze - Damp - Dry

Tense - Strong - Taut - Numb - Tingling - Tickling - Muscle - Slender - Fragile

Pressure - Throbbing - Blocked - Pulse - Stabbing - Quivering

Nauseous - Shaking - Aching - Breathless - Wired - Anxious

Soothed - Relaxed - Comfortable - Free Flowing

# Body Scan

Today's Date _____     Time _____

Where are you? _____

### Head and Face

### Chest

### Neck and Shoulders

### Stomach

### Spine

### Arms

### Hips and Pelvis

### Legs

### Whole body sensations

## Sensations

Warm - Cold - Soft - Hard -Breeze - Damp - Dry

Tense - Strong - Taut - Numb - Tingling - Tickling - Muscle - Slender - Fragile

Pressure - Throbbing - Blocked - Pulse - Stabbing - Quivering

Nauseous - Shaking - Aching - Breathless - Wired - Anxious

Soothed - Relaxed - Comfortable - Free Flowing

# Body Scan     Today's Date _____     Time _____

Where are you? _____

Head and Face

[ ]

Chest

[ ]

Neck and Shoulders

[ ]

Stomach

[ ]

Spine

[ ]

Arms

[ ]

Hips and Pelvis

[ ]

Legs

[ ]

Whole body sensations

[ ]

## Sensations

Warm - Cold - Soft - Hard -Breeze - Damp - Dry

Tense - Strong - Taut - Numb - Tingling - Tickling - Muscle - Slender - Fragile

Pressure - Throbbing - Blocked - Pulse - Stabbing - Quivering

Nauseous - Shaking - Aching - Breathless - Wired - Anxious

Soothed - Relaxed - Comfortable - Free Flowing

# Body Scan

Today's Date _____     Time _____

Where are you? _____

### Head and Face

### Chest

### Neck and Shoulders

### Stomach

### Spine

### Arms

### Hips and Pelvis

### Legs

### Whole body sensations

## Sensations

Warm - Cold - Soft - Hard -Breeze - Damp - Dry

Tense - Strong - Taut - Numb - Tingling - Tickling - Muscle - Slender - Fragile

Pressure - Throbbing - Blocked - Pulse - Stabbing - Quivering

Nauseous - Shaking - Aching - Breathless - Wired - Anxious

Soothed - Relaxed - Comfortable - Free Flowing

# Body Scan

Today's Date _____     Time _____

Where are you? _____

### Head and Face

```
[                              ]
```

### Chest

```
[                              ]
```

### Neck and Shoulders

```
[                              ]
```

### Stomach

```
[                              ]
```

### Spine

```
[                              ]
```

### Arms

```
[                              ]
```

### Hips and Pelvis

```
[                              ]
```

### Legs

```
[                              ]
```

### Whole body sensations

```
[                              ]
```

### Sensations

Warm - Cold - Soft - Hard -Breeze - Damp - Dry

Tense - Strong - Taut - Numb - Tingling - Tickling - Muscle - Slender - Fragile

Pressure - Throbbing - Blocked - Pulse - Stabbing - Quivering

Nauseous - Shaking - Aching - Breathless - Wired - Anxious

Soothed - Relaxed - Comfortable - Free Flowing

# Body Scan

Today's Date _____     Time _____

Where are you? _____

### Head and Face

### Chest

### Neck and Shoulders

### Stomach

### Spine

### Arms

### Hips and Pelvis

### Legs

### Whole body sensations

### Sensations

Warm - Cold - Soft - Hard -Breeze - Damp - Dry

Tense - Strong - Taut - Numb - Tingling - Tickling - Muscle - Slender - Fragile

Pressure - Throbbing - Blocked - Pulse - Stabbing - Quivering

Nauseous - Shaking - Aching - Breathless - Wired - Anxious

Soothed - Relaxed - Comfortable - Free Flowing

# Body Scan

Today's Date _____     Time _____

Where are you? _____

Head and Face

[ ]

Chest

[ ]

Neck and Shoulders

[ ]

Stomach

[ ]

Spine

[ ]

Arms

[ ]

Hips and Pelvis

[ ]

Legs

[ ]

Whole body sensations

[ ]

### Sensations

Warm - Cold - Soft - Hard -Breeze - Damp - Dry

Tense - Strong - Taut - Numb - Tingling - Tickling - Muscle - Slender - Fragile

Pressure - Throbbing - Blocked - Pulse - Stabbing - Quivering

Nauseous - Shaking - Aching - Breathless - Wired - Anxious

Soothed - Relaxed - Comfortable - Free Flowing

# Body Scan

Today's Date _____  Time _____

Where are you? _____

### Head and Face



### Chest



### Neck and Shoulders



### Stomach



### Spine



### Arms



### Hips and Pelvis



### Legs



### Whole body sensations



## Sensations

Warm - Cold - Soft - Hard - Breeze - Damp - Dry

Tense - Strong - Taut - Numb - Tingling - Tickling - Muscle - Slender - Fragile

Pressure - Throbbing - Blocked - Pulse - Stabbing - Quivering

Nauseous - Shaking - Aching - Breathless - Wired - Anxious

Soothed - Relaxed - Comfortable - Free Flowing

# Body Scan

Today's Date _____     Time _____

Where are you? _____

Head and Face

[ ]

Chest

[ ]

Neck and Shoulders

[ ]

Stomach

[ ]

Spine

[ ]

Arms

[ ]

Hips and Pelvis

[ ]

Legs

[ ]

Whole body sensations

[ ]

## Sensations

Warm - Cold - Soft - Hard -Breeze - Damp - Dry

Tense - Strong - Taut - Numb - Tingling - Tickling - Muscle - Slender - Fragile

Pressure - Throbbing - Blocked - Pulse - Stabbing - Quivering

Nauseous - Shaking - Aching - Breathless - Wired - Anxious

Soothed - Relaxed - Comfortable - Free Flowing

# Body Scan

Today's Date _____     Time _____

Where are you? _____

Head and Face

[ ]

Chest

[ ]

Neck and Shoulders

[ ]

Stomach

[ ]

Spine

[ ]

Arms

[ ]

Hips and Pelvis

[ ]

Legs

[ ]

Whole body sensations

[ ]

## Sensations

Warm - Cold - Soft - Hard -Breeze - Damp - Dry

Tense - Strong - Taut - Numb - Tingling - Tickling - Muscle - Slender - Fragile

Pressure - Throbbing - Blocked - Pulse - Stabbing - Quivering

Nauseous - Shaking - Aching - Breathless - Wired - Anxious

Soothed - Relaxed - Comfortable - Free Flowing

# Body Scan

Today's Date _____     Time _____

Where are you? _____

### Head and Face

```
[ ]
```

### Chest

```
[ ]
```

### Neck and Shoulders

```
[ ]
```

### Stomach

```
[ ]
```

### Spine

```
[ ]
```

### Arms

```
[ ]
```

### Hips and Pelvis

```
[ ]
```

### Legs

```
[ ]
```

### Whole body sensations

```
[ ]
```

## Sensations

Warm - Cold - Soft - Hard -Breeze - Damp - Dry

Tense - Strong - Taut - Numb - Tingling - Tickling - Muscle - Slender - Fragile

Pressure - Throbbing - Blocked - Pulse - Stabbing - Quivering

Nauseous - Shaking - Aching - Breathless - Wired - Anxious

Soothed - Relaxed - Comfortable - Free Flowing

# Body Scan

Today's Date _____     Time _____

Where are you?  _____

Head and Face

Chest

Neck and Shoulders

Stomach

Spine

Arms

Hips and Pelvis

Legs

Whole body sensations

### Sensations

Warm - Cold - Soft - Hard -Breeze - Damp - Dry

Tense - Strong - Taut - Numb - Tingling - Tickling - Muscle - Slender - Fragile

Pressure - Throbbing - Blocked - Pulse - Stabbing - Quivering

Nauseous - Shaking - Aching - Breathless - Wired - Anxious

Soothed - Relaxed - Comfortable - Free Flowing

# Body Scan

Today's Date _____     Time _____

Where are you? _____

## Head and Face

[ ]

## Chest

[ ]

## Neck and Shoulders

[ ]

## Stomach

[ ]

## Spine

[ ]

## Arms

[ ]

## Hips and Pelvis

[ ]

## Legs

[ ]

## Whole body sensations

[ ]

### Sensations

Warm - Cold - Soft - Hard -Breeze - Damp - Dry

Tense - Strong - Taut - Numb - Tingling - Tickling - Muscle - Slender - Fragile

Pressure - Throbbing - Blocked - Pulse - Stabbing - Quivering

Nauseous - Shaking - Aching - Breathless - Wired - Anxious

Soothed - Relaxed - Comfortable - Free Flowing

# Body Scan

Today's Date _____     Time _____

Where are you? _____

Head and Face

Chest

Neck and Shoulders

Stomach

Spine

Arms

Hips and Pelvis

Legs

Whole body sensations

Sensations

Warm - Cold - Soft - Hard -Breeze - Damp - Dry

Tense - Strong - Taut - Numb - Tingling - Tickling - Muscle - Slender - Fragile

Pressure - Throbbing - Blocked - Pulse - Stabbing - Quivering

Nauseous - Shaking - Aching - Breathless - Wired - Anxious

Soothed - Relaxed - Comfortable - Free Flowing

# Body Scan

Today's Date _____     Time _____

Where are you? _____

## Head and Face

## Chest

## Neck and Shoulders

## Stomach

## Spine

## Arms

## Hips and Pelvis

## Legs

## Whole body sensations

### Sensations

Warm - Cold - Soft - Hard -Breeze - Damp - Dry

Tense - Strong - Taut - Numb - Tingling - Tickling - Muscle - Slender - Fragile

Pressure - Throbbing - Blocked - Pulse - Stabbing - Quivering

Nauseous - Shaking - Aching - Breathless - Wired - Anxious

Soothed - Relaxed - Comfortable - Free Flowing

# Body Scan

Today's Date _____          Time _____

Where are you? _____

### Head and Face

[          ]

### Chest

[          ]

### Neck and Shoulders

[          ]

### Stomach

[          ]

### Spine

[          ]

### Arms

[          ]

### Hips and Pelvis

[          ]

### Legs

[          ]

### Whole body sensations

[          ]

### Sensations

Warm - Cold - Soft - Hard -Breeze - Damp - Dry

Tense - Strong - Taut - Numb - Tingling - Tickling - Muscle - Slender - Fragile

Pressure - Throbbing - Blocked - Pulse - Stabbing - Quivering

Nauseous - Shaking - Aching - Breathless - Wired - Anxious

Soothed - Relaxed - Comfortable - Free Flowing

# Body Scan

Today's Date _____ Time _____

Where are you? _____

Head and Face

Chest

Neck and Shoulders

Stomach

Spine

Arms

Hips and Pelvis

Legs

Whole body sensations

### Sensations

Warm - Cold - Soft - Hard -Breeze - Damp - Dry

Tense - Strong - Taut - Numb - Tingling - Tickling - Muscle - Slender - Fragile

Pressure - Throbbing - Blocked - Pulse - Stabbing - Quivering

Nauseous - Shaking - Aching - Breathless - Wired - Anxious

Soothed - Relaxed - Comfortable - Free Flowing

# Body Scan

Today's Date _____       Time _____

Where are you? _____

## Head and Face

```



```

## Chest

```



```

## Neck and Shoulders

```



```

## Stomach

```



```

## Spine

```



```

## Arms

```



```

## Hips and Pelvis

```



```

## Legs

```



```

## Whole body sensations

```



```

### Sensations

Warm - Cold - Soft - Hard -Breeze - Damp - Dry

Tense - Strong - Taut - Numb - Tingling - Tickling - Muscle - Slender - Fragile

Pressure - Throbbing - Blocked - Pulse - Stabbing - Quivering

Nauseous - Shaking - Aching - Breathless - Wired - Anxious

Soothed - Relaxed - Comfortable - Free Flowing

# Body Scan

Today's Date _____     Time _____

Where are you? _____

## Head and Face

## Chest

## Neck and Shoulders

## Stomach

## Spine

## Arms

## Hips and Pelvis

## Legs

## Whole body sensations

### Sensations

Warm - Cold - Soft - Hard -Breeze - Damp - Dry

Tense - Strong - Taut - Numb - Tingling - Tickling - Muscle - Slender - Fragile

Pressure - Throbbing - Blocked - Pulse - Stabbing - Quivering

Nauseous - Shaking - Aching - Breathless - Wired - Anxious

Soothed - Relaxed - Comfortable - Free Flowing

# Body Scan

Today's Date _____     Time _____

Where are you? _____

### Head and Face

### Chest

### Neck and Shoulders

### Stomach

### Spine

### Arms

### Hips and Pelvis

### Legs

### Whole body sensations

## Sensations

Warm - Cold - Soft - Hard -Breeze - Damp - Dry

Tense - Strong - Taut - Numb - Tingling - Tickling - Muscle - Slender - Fragile

Pressure - Throbbing - Blocked - Pulse - Stabbing - Quivering

Nauseous - Shaking - Aching - Breathless - Wired - Anxious

Soothed - Relaxed - Comfortable - Free Flowing

# Body Scan     Today's Date _____     Time _____

Where are you? _____

Head and Face

Chest

Neck and Shoulders

Stomach

Spine

Arms

Hips and Pelvis

Legs

Whole body sensations

## Sensations

Warm - Cold - Soft - Hard -Breeze - Damp - Dry

Tense - Strong - Taut - Numb - Tingling - Tickling - Muscle - Slender - Fragile

Pressure - Throbbing - Blocked - Pulse - Stabbing - Quivering

Nauseous - Shaking - Aching - Breathless - Wired - Anxious

Soothed - Relaxed - Comfortable - Free Flowing

# Body Scan

Today's Date _____     Time _____

Where are you? _____

### Head and Face

### Chest

### Neck and Shoulders

### Stomach

### Spine

### Arms

### Hips and Pelvis

### Legs

### Whole body sensations

### Sensations

Warm - Cold - Soft - Hard -Breeze - Damp - Dry

Tense - Strong - Taut - Numb - Tingling - Tickling - Muscle - Slender - Fragile

Pressure - Throbbing - Blocked - Pulse - Stabbing - Quivering

Nauseous - Shaking - Aching - Breathless - Wired - Anxious

Soothed - Relaxed - Comfortable - Free Flowing

# Body Scan

Today's Date _____     Time _____

Where are you? _____

## Head and Face

|  |
|--|
|  |

## Chest

|  |
|--|
|  |

## Neck and Shoulders

|  |
|--|
|  |

## Stomach

|  |
|--|
|  |

## Spine

|  |
|--|
|  |

## Arms

|  |
|--|
|  |

## Hips and Pelvis

|  |
|--|
|  |

## Legs

|  |
|--|
|  |

## Whole body sensations

|  |
|--|
|  |

### Sensations

Warm - Cold - Soft - Hard -Breeze - Damp - Dry

Tense - Strong - Taut - Numb - Tingling - Tickling - Muscle - Slender - Fragile

Pressure - Throbbing - Blocked - Pulse - Stabbing - Quivering

Nauseous - Shaking - Aching - Breathless - Wired - Anxious

Soothed - Relaxed - Comfortable - Free Flowing

# Body Scan

Today's Date _____     Time _____

Where are you? _____

Head and Face

_____

Chest

_____

Neck and Shoulders

_____

Stomach

_____

Spine

_____

Arms

_____

Hips and Pelvis

_____

Legs

_____

Whole body sensations

_____

## Sensations

Warm - Cold - Soft - Hard -Breeze - Damp - Dry

Tense - Strong - Taut - Numb - Tingling - Tickling - Muscle - Slender - Fragile

Pressure - Throbbing - Blocked - Pulse - Stabbing - Quivering

Nauseous - Shaking - Aching - Breathless - Wired - Anxious

Soothed - Relaxed - Comfortable - Free Flowing

# Body Scan

Today's Date _____     Time _____

Where are you? _____

### Head and Face

[ ]

### Chest

[ ]

### Neck and Shoulders

[ ]

### Stomach

[ ]

### Spine

[ ]

### Arms

[ ]

### Hips and Pelvis

[ ]

### Legs

[ ]

### Whole body sensations

[ ]

### Sensations

Warm - Cold - Soft - Hard - Breeze - Damp - Dry

Tense - Strong - Taut - Numb - Tingling - Tickling - Muscle - Slender - Fragile

Pressure - Throbbing - Blocked - Pulse - Stabbing - Quivering

Nauseous - Shaking - Aching - Breathless - Wired - Anxious

Soothed - Relaxed - Comfortable - Free Flowing

# Body Scan

Today's Date _____ Time _____

Where are you? _____

Head and Face

Chest

Neck and Shoulders

Stomach

Spine

Arms

Hips and Pelvis

Legs

Whole body sensations

### Sensations

Warm - Cold - Soft - Hard -Breeze - Damp - Dry

Tense - Strong - Taut - Numb - Tingling - Tickling - Muscle - Slender - Fragile

Pressure - Throbbing - Blocked - Pulse - Stabbing - Quivering

Nauseous - Shaking - Aching - Breathless - Wired - Anxious

Soothed - Relaxed - Comfortable - Free Flowing

# Body Scan

Today's Date _____     Time _____

Where are you? _____

### Head and Face

[ ]

### Chest

[ ]

### Neck and Shoulders

[ ]

### Stomach

[ ]

### Spine

[ ]

### Arms

[ ]

### Hips and Pelvis

[ ]

### Legs

[ ]

### Whole body sensations

[ ]

## Sensations

Warm - Cold - Soft - Hard -Breeze - Damp - Dry

Tense - Strong - Taut - Numb - Tingling - Tickling - Muscle - Slender - Fragile

Pressure - Throbbing - Blocked - Pulse - Stabbing - Quivering

Nauseous - Shaking - Aching - Breathless - Wired - Anxious

Soothed - Relaxed - Comfortable - Free Flowing

# Body Scan

Today's Date _____       Time _____

Where are you? _____

### Head and Face

_(blank box)_

### Neck and Shoulders

_(blank box)_

### Spine

_(blank box)_

### Hips and Pelvis

_(blank box)_

### Chest

_(blank box)_

### Stomach

_(blank box)_

### Arms

_(blank box)_

### Legs

_(blank box)_

### Whole body sensations

_(blank box)_

## Sensations

Warm - Cold - Soft - Hard -Breeze - Damp - Dry

Tense - Strong - Taut - Numb - Tingling - Tickling - Muscle - Slender - Fragile

Pressure - Throbbing - Blocked - Pulse - Stabbing - Quivering

Nauseous - Shaking - Aching - Breathless - Wired - Anxious

Soothed - Relaxed - Comfortable - Free Flowing

# Body Scan

Today's Date _____     Time _____

Where are you? _____

### Head and Face

### Chest

### Neck and Shoulders

### Stomach

### Spine

### Arms

### Hips and Pelvis

### Legs

### Whole body sensations

## Sensations

Warm - Cold - Soft - Hard -Breeze - Damp - Dry

Tense - Strong - Taut - Numb - Tingling - Tickling - Muscle - Slender - Fragile

Pressure - Throbbing - Blocked - Pulse - Stabbing - Quivering

Nauseous - Shaking - Aching - Breathless - Wired - Anxious

Soothed - Relaxed - Comfortable - Free Flowing

# Body Scan

Today's Date _____      Time _____

Where are you? _____

### Head and Face

_(blank box)_

### Chest

_(blank box)_

### Neck and Shoulders

_(blank box)_

### Stomach

_(blank box)_

### Spine

_(blank box)_

### Arms

_(blank box)_

### Hips and Pelvis

_(blank box)_

### Legs

_(blank box)_

### Whole body sensations

_(blank box)_

## Sensations

Warm - Cold - Soft - Hard -Breeze - Damp - Dry

Tense - Strong - Taut - Numb - Tingling - Tickling - Muscle - Slender - Fragile

Pressure - Throbbing - Blocked - Pulse - Stabbing - Quivering

Nauseous - Shaking - Aching - Breathless - Wired - Anxious

Soothed - Relaxed - Comfortable - Free Flowing

# Body Scan

Today's Date _____     Time _____

Where are you? _____

Head and Face

┌─────────────────────────┐
│                         │
│                         │
│                         │
└─────────────────────────┘

Chest

┌─────────────────────────┐
│                         │
│                         │
│                         │
└─────────────────────────┘

Neck and Shoulders

┌─────────────────────────┐
│                         │
│                         │
│                         │
└─────────────────────────┘

Stomach

┌─────────────────────────┐
│                         │
│                         │
│                         │
└─────────────────────────┘

Spine

┌─────────────────────────┐
│                         │
│                         │
│                         │
└─────────────────────────┘

Arms

┌─────────────────────────┐
│                         │
│                         │
│                         │
└─────────────────────────┘

Hips and Pelvis

┌─────────────────────────┐
│                         │
│                         │
│                         │
└─────────────────────────┘

Legs

┌─────────────────────────┐
│                         │
│                         │
│                         │
└─────────────────────────┘

Whole body sensations

┌───────────────────────────────────────────────────────┐
│                                                         │
│                                                         │
│                                                         │
└───────────────────────────────────────────────────────┘

Sensations

Warm - Cold - Soft - Hard -Breeze - Damp - Dry

Tense - Strong - Taut - Numb - Tingling - Tickling - Muscle - Slender - Fragile

Pressure - Throbbing - Blocked - Pulse - Stabbing - Quivering

Nauseous - Shaking - Aching - Breathless - Wired - Anxious

Soothed - Relaxed - Comfortable - Free Flowing

# Body Scan

Today's Date _____    Time _____

Where are you? _____

### Head and Face

_(blank box)_

### Chest

_(blank box)_

### Neck and Shoulders

_(blank box)_

### Stomach

_(blank box)_

### Spine

_(blank box)_

### Arms

_(blank box)_

### Hips and Pelvis

_(blank box)_

### Legs

_(blank box)_

### Whole body sensations

_(blank box)_

### Sensations

Warm - Cold - Soft - Hard -Breeze - Damp - Dry

Tense - Strong - Taut - Numb - Tingling - Tickling - Muscle - Slender - Fragile

Pressure - Throbbing - Blocked - Pulse - Stabbing - Quivering

Nauseous - Shaking - Aching - Breathless - Wired - Anxious

Soothed - Relaxed - Comfortable - Free Flowing

# Body Scan

Today's Date _____      Time _____

Where are you? _____

Head and Face

[ ]

Chest

[ ]

Neck and Shoulders

[ ]

Stomach

[ ]

Spine

[ ]

Arms

[ ]

Hips and Pelvis

[ ]

Legs

[ ]

Whole body sensations

[ ]

## Sensations

Warm - Cold - Soft - Hard -Breeze - Damp - Dry

Tense - Strong - Taut - Numb - Tingling - Tickling - Muscle - Slender - Fragile

Pressure - Throbbing - Blocked - Pulse - Stabbing - Quivering

Nauseous - Shaking - Aching - Breathless - Wired - Anxious

Soothed - Relaxed - Comfortable - Free Flowing

# Body Scan

Today's Date _____     Time _____

Where are you? _____

### Head and Face

[ ]

### Chest

[ ]

### Neck and Shoulders

[ ]

### Stomach

[ ]

### Spine

[ ]

### Arms

[ ]

### Hips and Pelvis

[ ]

### Legs

[ ]

### Whole body sensations

[ ]

### Sensations

Warm - Cold - Soft - Hard -Breeze - Damp - Dry

Tense - Strong - Taut - Numb - Tingling - Tickling - Muscle - Slender - Fragile

Pressure - Throbbing - Blocked - Pulse - Stabbing - Quivering

Nauseous - Shaking - Aching - Breathless - Wired - Anxious

Soothed - Relaxed - Comfortable - Free Flowing

# Body Scan

Today's Date _____    Time _____

Where are you? _____

Head and Face

[ ]

Chest

[ ]

Neck and Shoulders

[ ]

Stomach

[ ]

Spine

[ ]

Arms

[ ]

Hips and Pelvis

[ ]

Legs

[ ]

Whole body sensations

[ ]

Sensations

Warm - Cold - Soft - Hard -Breeze - Damp - Dry

Tense - Strong - Taut - Numb - Tingling - Tickling - Muscle - Slender - Fragile

Pressure - Throbbing - Blocked - Pulse - Stabbing - Quivering

Nauseous - Shaking - Aching - Breathless - Wired - Anxious

Soothed - Relaxed - Comfortable - Free Flowing

# Body Scan

Today's Date _____    Time _____

Where are you? _____

### Head and Face

### Chest

### Neck and Shoulders

### Stomach

### Spine

### Arms

### Hips and Pelvis

### Legs

### Whole body sensations

## Sensations

Warm - Cold - Soft - Hard -Breeze - Damp - Dry

Tense - Strong - Taut - Numb - Tingling - Tickling - Muscle - Slender - Fragile

Pressure - Throbbing - Blocked - Pulse - Stabbing - Quivering

Nauseous - Shaking - Aching - Breathless - Wired - Anxious

Soothed - Relaxed - Comfortable - Free Flowing

# Body Scan

Today's Date _____     Time _____

Where are you? _____

### Head and Face

[   ]

### Chest

[   ]

### Neck and Shoulders

[   ]

### Stomach

[   ]

### Spine

[   ]

### Arms

[   ]

### Hips and Pelvis

[   ]

### Legs

[   ]

### Whole body sensations

[   ]

## Sensations

Warm - Cold - Soft - Hard -Breeze - Damp - Dry

Tense - Strong - Taut - Numb - Tingling - Tickling - Muscle - Slender - Fragile

Pressure - Throbbing - Blocked - Pulse - Stabbing - Quivering

Nauseous - Shaking - Aching - Breathless - Wired - Anxious

Soothed - Relaxed - Comfortable - Free Flowing

# Body Scan

Today's Date _____     Time _____

Where are you? _____

Head and Face

[ ]

Chest

[ ]

Neck and Shoulders

[ ]

Stomach

[ ]

Spine

[ ]

Arms

[ ]

Hips and Pelvis

[ ]

Legs

[ ]

Whole body sensations

[ ]

Sensations

Warm - Cold - Soft - Hard -Breeze - Damp - Dry

Tense - Strong - Taut - Numb - Tingling - Tickling - Muscle - Slender - Fragile

Pressure - Throbbing - Blocked - Pulse - Stabbing - Quivering

Nauseous - Shaking - Aching - Breathless - Wired - Anxious

Soothed - Relaxed - Comfortable - Free Flowing

# Body Scan

Today's Date _____    Time _____

Where are you? _____

Head and Face

Chest

Neck and Shoulders

Stomach

Spine

Arms

Hips and Pelvis

Legs

Whole body sensations

### Sensations

Warm - Cold - Soft - Hard -Breeze - Damp - Dry

Tense - Strong - Taut - Numb - Tingling - Tickling - Muscle - Slender - Fragile

Pressure - Throbbing - Blocked - Pulse - Stabbing - Quivering

Nauseous - Shaking - Aching - Breathless - Wired - Anxious

Soothed - Relaxed - Comfortable - Free Flowing

# Body Scan

Today's Date _____    Time _____

Where are you? _____

Head and Face

[ ]

Chest

[ ]

Neck and Shoulders

[ ]

Stomach

[ ]

Spine

[ ]

Arms

[ ]

Hips and Pelvis

[ ]

Legs

[ ]

Whole body sensations

[ ]

### Sensations

Warm - Cold - Soft - Hard -Breeze - Damp - Dry

Tense - Strong - Taut - Numb - Tingling - Tickling - Muscle - Slender - Fragile

Pressure - Throbbing - Blocked - Pulse - Stabbing - Quivering

Nauseous - Shaking - Aching - Breathless - Wired - Anxious

Soothed - Relaxed - Comfortable - Free Flowing

# Body Scan

Today's Date _____     Time _____

Where are you? _____

### Head and Face

### Chest

### Neck and Shoulders

### Stomach

### Spine

### Arms

### Hips and Pelvis

### Legs

### Whole body sensations

## Sensations

Warm - Cold - Soft - Hard -Breeze - Damp - Dry

Tense - Strong - Taut - Numb - Tingling - Tickling - Muscle - Slender - Fragile

Pressure - Throbbing - Blocked - Pulse - Stabbing - Quivering

Nauseous - Shaking - Aching - Breathless - Wired - Anxious

Soothed - Relaxed - Comfortable - Free Flowing

# Body Scan

Today's Date _____          Time _____

Where are you? _____

### Head and Face

### Chest

### Neck and Shoulders

### Stomach

### Spine

### Arms

### Hips and Pelvis

### Legs

### Whole body sensations

### Sensations

Warm - Cold - Soft - Hard - Breeze - Damp - Dry

Tense - Strong - Taut - Numb - Tingling - Tickling - Muscle - Slender - Fragile

Pressure - Throbbing - Blocked - Pulse - Stabbing - Quivering

Nauseous - Shaking - Aching - Breathless - Wired - Anxious

Soothed - Relaxed - Comfortable - Free Flowing

# Body Scan

Today's Date _____     Time _____

Where are you? _____

### Head and Face

### Chest

### Neck and Shoulders

### Stomach

### Spine

### Arms

### Hips and Pelvis

### Legs

### Whole body sensations

## Sensations

Warm - Cold - Soft - Hard -Breeze - Damp - Dry

Tense - Strong - Taut - Numb - Tingling - Tickling - Muscle - Slender - Fragile

Pressure - Throbbing - Blocked - Pulse - Stabbing - Quivering

Nauseous - Shaking - Aching - Breathless - Wired - Anxious

Soothed - Relaxed - Comfortable - Free Flowing

# Body Scan

Today's Date _____     Time _____

Where are you? _____

### Head and Face

### Chest

### Neck and Shoulders

### Stomach

### Spine

### Arms

### Hips and Pelvis

### Legs

### Whole body sensations

## Sensations

Warm - Cold - Soft - Hard -Breeze - Damp - Dry

Tense - Strong - Taut - Numb - Tingling - Tickling - Muscle - Slender - Fragile

Pressure - Throbbing - Blocked - Pulse - Stabbing - Quivering

Nauseous - Shaking - Aching - Breathless - Wired - Anxious

Soothed - Relaxed - Comfortable - Free Flowing

# Body Scan

Today's Date _____     Time _____

Where are you? _____

### Head and Face

[  ]

### Chest

[  ]

### Neck and Shoulders

[  ]

### Stomach

[  ]

### Spine

[  ]

### Arms

[  ]

### Hips and Pelvis

[  ]

### Legs

[  ]

### Whole body sensations

[  ]

## Sensations

Warm - Cold - Soft - Hard -Breeze - Damp - Dry

Tense - Strong - Taut - Numb - Tingling - Tickling - Muscle - Slender - Fragile

Pressure - Throbbing - Blocked - Pulse - Stabbing - Quivering

Nauseous - Shaking - Aching - Breathless - Wired - Anxious

Soothed - Relaxed - Comfortable - Free Flowing

# Body Scan

Today's Date _____     Time _____

Where are you? _____

### Head and Face

[ ]

### Chest

[ ]

### Neck and Shoulders

[ ]

### Stomach

[ ]

### Spine

[ ]

### Arms

[ ]

### Hips and Pelvis

[ ]

### Legs

[ ]

### Whole body sensations

[ ]

### Sensations

Warm - Cold - Soft - Hard -Breeze - Damp - Dry

Tense - Strong - Taut - Numb - Tingling - Tickling - Muscle - Slender - Fragile

Pressure - Throbbing - Blocked - Pulse - Stabbing - Quivering

Nauseous - Shaking - Aching - Breathless - Wired - Anxious

Soothed - Relaxed - Comfortable - Free Flowing

# Body Scan

Today's Date _____     Time _____

Where are you? _____

### Head and Face

[ ]

### Chest

[ ]

### Neck and Shoulders

[ ]

### Stomach

[ ]

### Spine

[ ]

### Arms

[ ]

### Hips and Pelvis

[ ]

### Legs

[ ]

### Whole body sensations

[ ]

## Sensations

Warm - Cold - Soft - Hard -Breeze - Damp - Dry

Tense - Strong - Taut - Numb - Tingling - Tickling - Muscle - Slender - Fragile

Pressure - Throbbing - Blocked - Pulse - Stabbing - Quivering

Nauseous - Shaking - Aching - Breathless - Wired - Anxious

Soothed - Relaxed - Comfortable - Free Flowing

# Body Scan

Today's Date _____    Time _____

Where are you? _____

## Head and Face

## Chest

## Neck and Shoulders

## Stomach

## Spine

## Arms

## Hips and Pelvis

## Legs

## Whole body sensations

### Sensations

Warm - Cold - Soft - Hard -Breeze - Damp - Dry

Tense - Strong - Taut - Numb - Tingling - Tickling - Muscle - Slender - Fragile

Pressure - Throbbing - Blocked - Pulse - Stabbing - Quivering

Nauseous - Shaking - Aching - Breathless - Wired - Anxious

Soothed - Relaxed - Comfortable - Free Flowing

# Body Scan

Today's Date _____     Time _____

Where are you? _____

**Head and Face**

**Chest**

**Neck and Shoulders**

**Stomach**

**Spine**

**Arms**

**Hips and Pelvis**

**Legs**

**Whole body sensations**

## Sensations

Warm - Cold - Soft - Hard -Breeze - Damp - Dry

Tense - Strong - Taut - Numb - Tingling - Tickling - Muscle - Slender - Fragile

Pressure - Throbbing - Blocked - Pulse - Stabbing - Quivering

Nauseous - Shaking - Aching - Breathless - Wired - Anxious

Soothed - Relaxed - Comfortable - Free Flowing

# Body Scan

Today's Date _____     Time _____

Where are you? _____

## Head and Face

## Chest

## Neck and Shoulders

## Stomach

## Spine

## Arms

## Hips and Pelvis

## Legs

## Whole body sensations

### Sensations

Warm - Cold - Soft - Hard -Breeze - Damp - Dry

Tense - Strong - Taut - Numb - Tingling - Tickling - Muscle - Slender - Fragile

Pressure - Throbbing - Blocked - Pulse - Stabbing - Quivering

Nauseous - Shaking - Aching - Breathless - Wired - Anxious

Soothed - Relaxed - Comfortable - Free Flowing

# Body Scan

Today's Date _____     Time _____

Where are you? _____

Head and Face

[ ]

Chest

[ ]

Neck and Shoulders

[ ]

Stomach

[ ]

Spine

[ ]

Arms

[ ]

Hips and Pelvis

[ ]

Legs

[ ]

Whole body sensations

[ ]

## Sensations

Warm - Cold - Soft - Hard -Breeze - Damp - Dry

Tense - Strong - Taut - Numb - Tingling - Tickling - Muscle - Slender - Fragile

Pressure - Throbbing - Blocked - Pulse - Stabbing - Quivering

Nauseous - Shaking - Aching - Breathless - Wired - Anxious

Soothed - Relaxed - Comfortable - Free Flowing

# Body Scan

Today's Date _____     Time _____

Where are you? _____

### Head and Face

[ ]

### Chest

[ ]

### Neck and Shoulders

[ ]

### Stomach

[ ]

### Spine

[ ]

### Arms

[ ]

### Hips and Pelvis

[ ]

### Legs

[ ]

### Whole body sensations

[ ]

### Sensations

Warm - Cold - Soft - Hard -Breeze - Damp - Dry

Tense - Strong - Taut - Numb - Tingling - Tickling - Muscle - Slender - Fragile

Pressure - Throbbing - Blocked - Pulse - Stabbing - Quivering

Nauseous - Shaking - Aching - Breathless - Wired - Anxious

Soothed - Relaxed - Comfortable - Free Flowing

# Body Scan

Today's Date _____        Time _____

Where are you? _____

## Head and Face

[ ]

## Chest

[ ]

## Neck and Shoulders

[ ]

## Stomach

[ ]

## Spine

[ ]

## Arms

[ ]

## Hips and Pelvis

[ ]

## Legs

[ ]

## Whole body sensations

[ ]

### Sensations

Warm - Cold - Soft - Hard -Breeze - Damp - Dry

Tense - Strong - Taut - Numb - Tingling - Tickling - Muscle - Slender - Fragile

Pressure - Throbbing - Blocked - Pulse - Stabbing - Quivering

Nauseous - Shaking - Aching - Breathless - Wired - Anxious

Soothed - Relaxed - Comfortable - Free Flowing

# Body Scan

Today's Date _____    Time _____

Where are you? _____

### Head and Face

### Chest

### Neck and Shoulders

### Stomach

### Spine

### Arms

### Hips and Pelvis

### Legs

### Whole body sensations

### Sensations

Warm - Cold - Soft - Hard - Breeze - Damp - Dry

Tense - Strong - Taut - Numb - Tingling - Tickling - Muscle - Slender - Fragile

Pressure - Throbbing - Blocked - Pulse - Stabbing - Quivering

Nauseous - Shaking - Aching - Breathless - Wired - Anxious

Soothed - Relaxed - Comfortable - Free Flowing

# Body Scan

Today's Date _____     Time _____

Where are you? _____

Head and Face

Neck and Shoulders

Spine

Hips and Pelvis

Chest

Stomach

Arms

Legs

Whole body sensations

### Sensations

Warm - Cold - Soft - Hard -Breeze - Damp - Dry

Tense - Strong - Taut - Numb - Tingling - Tickling - Muscle - Slender - Fragile

Pressure - Throbbing - Blocked - Pulse - Stabbing - Quivering

Nauseous - Shaking - Aching - Breathless - Wired - Anxious

Soothed - Relaxed - Comfortable - Free Flowing

# Body Scan

Today's Date _____  Time _____

Where are you? _____

Head and Face

Chest

Neck and Shoulders

Stomach

Spine

Arms

Hips and Pelvis

Legs

Whole body sensations

### Sensations

Warm - Cold - Soft - Hard -Breeze - Damp - Dry

Tense - Strong - Taut - Numb - Tingling - Tickling - Muscle - Slender - Fragile

Pressure - Throbbing - Blocked - Pulse - Stabbing - Quivering

Nauseous - Shaking - Aching - Breathless - Wired - Anxious

Soothed - Relaxed - Comfortable - Free Flowing

# Body Scan

Today's Date _____      Time _____

Where are you? _____

Head and Face

[ ]

Chest

[ ]

Neck and Shoulders

[ ]

Stomach

[ ]

Spine

[ ]

Arms

[ ]

Hips and Pelvis

[ ]

Legs

[ ]

Whole body sensations

[ ]

Sensations

Warm - Cold - Soft - Hard -Breeze - Damp - Dry

Tense - Strong - Taut - Numb - Tingling - Tickling - Muscle - Slender - Fragile

Pressure - Throbbing - Blocked - Pulse - Stabbing - Quivering

Nauseous - Shaking - Aching - Breathless - Wired - Anxious

Soothed - Relaxed - Comfortable - Free Flowing

# Body Scan

Today's Date _____    Time _____

Where are you? _____

### Head and Face

[ ]

### Chest

[ ]

### Neck and Shoulders

[ ]

### Stomach

[ ]

### Spine

[ ]

### Arms

[ ]

### Hips and Pelvis

[ ]

### Legs

[ ]

### Whole body sensations

[ ]

## Sensations

Warm - Cold - Soft - Hard -Breeze - Damp - Dry

Tense - Strong - Taut - Numb - Tingling - Tickling - Muscle - Slender - Fragile

Pressure - Throbbing - Blocked - Pulse - Stabbing - Quivering

Nauseous - Shaking - Aching - Breathless - Wired - Anxious

Soothed - Relaxed - Comfortable - Free Flowing

# Body Scan

Today's Date _____     Time _____

Where are you? _____

### Head and Face

<br><br><br>

### Chest

<br><br><br>

### Neck and Shoulders

<br><br><br>

### Stomach

<br><br><br>

### Spine

<br><br><br>

### Arms

<br><br><br>

### Hips and Pelvis

<br><br><br>

### Legs

<br><br><br>

### Whole body sensations

<br><br><br><br>

### Sensations

Warm - Cold - Soft - Hard -Breeze - Damp - Dry

Tense - Strong - Taut - Numb - Tingling - Tickling - Muscle - Slender - Fragile

Pressure - Throbbing - Blocked - Pulse - Stabbing - Quivering

Nauseous - Shaking - Aching - Breathless - Wired - Anxious

Soothed - Relaxed - Comfortable - Free Flowing

# Body Scan

Today's Date _____    Time _____

Where are you? _____

### Head and Face

### Chest

### Neck and Shoulders

### Stomach

### Spine

### Arms

### Hips and Pelvis

### Legs

### Whole body sensations

### Sensations

Warm - Cold - Soft - Hard -Breeze - Damp - Dry

Tense - Strong - Taut - Numb - Tingling - Tickling - Muscle - Slender - Fragile

Pressure - Throbbing - Blocked - Pulse - Stabbing - Quivering

Nauseous - Shaking - Aching - Breathless - Wired - Anxious

Soothed - Relaxed - Comfortable - Free Flowing

# Body Scan

Today's Date _____    Time _____

Where are you? _____

Head and Face

Chest

Neck and Shoulders

Stomach

Spine

Arms

Hips and Pelvis

Legs

Whole body sensations

### Sensations

Warm - Cold - Soft - Hard - Breeze - Damp - Dry

Tense - Strong - Taut - Numb - Tingling - Tickling - Muscle - Slender - Fragile

Pressure - Throbbing - Blocked - Pulse - Stabbing - Quivering

Nauseous - Shaking - Aching - Breathless - Wired - Anxious

Soothed - Relaxed - Comfortable - Free Flowing

# Body Scan

Today's Date _____     Time _____

Where are you? _____

## Head and Face

## Chest

## Neck and Shoulders

## Stomach

## Spine

## Arms

## Hips and Pelvis

## Legs

## Whole body sensations

### Sensations

Warm - Cold - Soft - Hard -Breeze - Damp - Dry

Tense - Strong - Taut - Numb - Tingling - Tickling - Muscle - Slender - Fragile

Pressure - Throbbing - Blocked - Pulse - Stabbing - Quivering

Nauseous - Shaking - Aching - Breathless - Wired - Anxious

Soothed - Relaxed - Comfortable - Free Flowing

# Body Scan   Today's Date _____   Time _____

Where are you? _____

Head and Face

[ ]

Chest

[ ]

Neck and Shoulders

[ ]

Stomach

[ ]

Spine

[ ]

Arms

[ ]

Hips and Pelvis

[ ]

Legs

[ ]

Whole body sensations

[ ]

## Sensations

Warm - Cold - Soft - Hard -Breeze - Damp - Dry

Tense - Strong - Taut - Numb - Tingling - Tickling - Muscle - Slender - Fragile

Pressure - Throbbing - Blocked - Pulse - Stabbing - Quivering

Nauseous - Shaking - Aching - Breathless - Wired - Anxious

Soothed - Relaxed - Comfortable - Free Flowing

# Body Scan

Today's Date _____     Time _____

Where are you? _____

### Head and Face

[ ]

### Chest

[ ]

### Neck and Shoulders

[ ]

### Stomach

[ ]

### Spine

[ ]

### Arms

[ ]

### Hips and Pelvis

[ ]

### Legs

[ ]

### Whole body sensations

[ ]

## Sensations

Warm - Cold - Soft - Hard -Breeze - Damp - Dry

Tense - Strong - Taut - Numb - Tingling - Tickling - Muscle - Slender - Fragile

Pressure - Throbbing - Blocked - Pulse - Stabbing - Quivering

Nauseous - Shaking - Aching - Breathless - Wired - Anxious

Soothed - Relaxed - Comfortable - Free Flowing

# Body Scan

Today's Date _____     Time _____

Where are you? _____

### Head and Face

### Chest

### Neck and Shoulders

### Stomach

### Spine

### Arms

### Hips and Pelvis

### Legs

### Whole body sensations

### Sensations

Warm - Cold - Soft - Hard -Breeze - Damp - Dry

Tense - Strong - Taut - Numb - Tingling - Tickling - Muscle - Slender - Fragile

Pressure - Throbbing - Blocked - Pulse - Stabbing - Quivering

Nauseous - Shaking - Aching - Breathless - Wired - Anxious

Soothed - Relaxed - Comfortable - Free Flowing

# Body Scan

Today's Date _____     Time _____

Where are you? _____

### Head and Face

### Chest

### Neck and Shoulders

### Stomach

### Spine

### Arms

### Hips and Pelvis

### Legs

### Whole body sensations

## Sensations

Warm - Cold - Soft - Hard -Breeze - Damp - Dry

Tense - Strong - Taut - Numb - Tingling - Tickling - Muscle - Slender - Fragile

Pressure - Throbbing - Blocked - Pulse - Stabbing - Quivering

Nauseous - Shaking - Aching - Breathless - Wired - Anxious

Soothed - Relaxed - Comfortable - Free Flowing

# Body Scan

Today's Date _____    Time _____

Where are you? _____

### Head and Face

[ ]

### Chest

[ ]

### Neck and Shoulders

[ ]

### Stomach

[ ]

### Spine

[ ]

### Arms

[ ]

### Hips and Pelvis

[ ]

### Legs

[ ]

### Whole body sensations

[ ]

Sensations

Warm - Cold - Soft - Hard -Breeze - Damp - Dry

Tense - Strong - Taut - Numb - Tingling - Tickling - Muscle - Slender - Fragile

Pressure - Throbbing - Blocked - Pulse - Stabbing - Quivering

Nauseous - Shaking - Aching - Breathless - Wired - Anxious

Soothed - Relaxed - Comfortable - Free Flowing

# Body Scan

Today's Date _____     Time _____

Where are you? _____

### Head and Face

### Chest

### Neck and Shoulders

### Stomach

### Spine

### Arms

### Hips and Pelvis

### Legs

### Whole body sensations

## Sensations

Warm - Cold - Soft - Hard -Breeze - Damp - Dry

Tense - Strong - Taut - Numb - Tingling - Tickling - Muscle - Slender - Fragile

Pressure - Throbbing - Blocked - Pulse - Stabbing - Quivering

Nauseous - Shaking - Aching - Breathless - Wired - Anxious

Soothed - Relaxed - Comfortable - Free Flowing

# Body Scan

Today's Date _____     Time _____

Where are you? _____

Head and Face

[ ]

Chest

[ ]

Neck and Shoulders

[ ]

Stomach

[ ]

Spine

[ ]

Arms

[ ]

Hips and Pelvis

[ ]

Legs

[ ]

Whole body sensations

[ ]

Sensations

Warm - Cold - Soft - Hard -Breeze - Damp - Dry

Tense - Strong - Taut - Numb - Tingling - Tickling - Muscle - Slender - Fragile

Pressure - Throbbing - Blocked - Pulse - Stabbing - Quivering

Nauseous - Shaking - Aching - Breathless - Wired - Anxious

Soothed - Relaxed - Comfortable - Free Flowing

Printed in Great Britain
by Amazon

84505479R00047